CERTIFIED
SCRUM
MASTER

EXAM Q & A

A complete study guide for getting the certified
scrum master certification, including thorough
test questions, exam tips, benefits, and correct
answers.

Bruce M. Chapman

ALL RIGHT RESERVED @ 2023

Bruce M. Chapman

Preface

Welcome to the " certified scrum master Exam Q & A: A complete study guide for getting the certified scrum master certification, including thorough test questions, exam tips, benefits, and correct answers." This beautifully crafted book serves as a thorough guide for individuals who are getting ready for the CSM exam. The bundle comprises a comprehensive study guide, practice exams, and a diverse selection of essay topics to enrich comprehension and proficiency in the subject. Additionally, it offers essential guidance and viewpoints to acquire a competitive advantage.

Forward

The CSM Exam Involving a rigorous assessment demanding profound comprehension of methodologies and values of Scrum, This book is the result of thorough research and ample expertise, assisting students in their exam preparation. The program aims to provide you with crucial knowledge and tools, guaranteeing both successful completion of the exam and a deep comprehension of the underlying core principles.

Introduction

In this book, You'll Explore a curated compilation of meticulously designed practice exams that faithfully replicate the structure and content of the authentic test. These tests familiarize you with the format of the examination and different question formats. Furthermore, the book has a wide range of essay topics that cover various aspects of CSM, encouraging intellectual engagement to enhance understanding at a deeper level.

In addition, it provides exceptional guidance and valuable insights carefully selected from accomplished specialists in the field. These strategies ensure a thorough comprehension of the exam's content and the most effective methods to tackle it.

This book is an indispensable tool that can greatly aid you in attaining success in the CSM Exam. May you attain outstanding outcomes in your academic pursuits and examinations, keeping in mind that triumph is certain upon the completion of this endeavor. The key element lies in initiating the initial actions—we shall begin!

TIPS FOR THE CSM EXAM:

1. **Understand the CSM Framework:** The CSM Exam necessitates a comprehensive comprehension of the core concepts, principles, and terminology that are inherent in the CSM framework. Ensure that you possess a thorough understanding of these components.

2. **PracticePractice with Mock Exams:** Mock tests provide a useful opportunity to acquaint oneself with the exam structure and experience diverse question formats. Moreover, they assist in identifying areas where you may need to augment your talents or abilities.

3. **Review the Syllabus:** Make sure you possess a thorough comprehension of the CSM Exam syllabus. This will allow you to focus your study efforts on the subjects that are most likely to be included in the examination.

4. **Arrange Your Time:** To effectively manage time during the CSM Exam and ensure timely completion of all questions, it is important to

have proficient time management skills within the specified time limit.

5. **Stay Calm and Focused:** Experiencing anxiety prior to an examination is a common occurrence, however, having a composed and focused mindset can enhance your performance.

BENEFITS OF THE CSM EXAM

1. **Expanded Proficiency:** The Certified Scrum Master (CSM) examination provides professionals with a thorough comprehension of Scrum concepts and agile practices, augmenting their proficiency to adeptly navigate and contribute to agile projects.

2. **Enhanced job prospects**: The CSM certification is highly regarded in the business, enhancing the attractiveness of certified persons to companies who are looking for proficient practitioners in agile frameworks. It can provide access to a wide range of employment prospects in project management and agile development.

3. **Collaboration among team member**s: CSM-certified persons are more adept at promoting collaboration among teams by acquiring a deep understanding of Scrum practices. This promotes a culture characterized by efficient communication, enhanced production, and a mutual comprehension of project objectives.

4. **Achievement of Project Objectives**: The CSM certification underscores the significance of iterative development and continual improvement, hence enhancing the probability of project success. Professionals has superior skills and resources to

effectively guide teams in providing relevant and top-notch products to stakeholders.

5. **Worldwide Acknowledgment:** The CSM certification is widely acknowledged worldwide, offering professionals a highly regarded certificate that is valued in various industries and regions. This acknowledgment might be advantageous for individuals operating in varied and global project settings.

1. In what way is a _____ developed in the second half of the sprint planning meeting and a _____ created in the first?

    A. Sprint Backlog, collection of tasks

    B. Product Backlog, collection of tasks

    C. Sprint Goal, Sprint Backlog

    D. Product Backlog, Sprint Backlog

Answer : **C**

2. How many sections make up the sprint planning meeting?

A. 4

B. 3

C. 2

D. 1

Answer : C

3. How long may each segment of a sprint planning meeting last?

A. 1 hour

B. 30 minutes

C. 4 hours

D. 2 hours

E. 15 minutes

Answer : **C**

4. Which of the following is the most recent Scrum framework phase, based on the activities listed?

    A. Daily scrum

    B. Sprint retrospective

    C. Sprint review

    D. Sprint planning

Answer : **B**

5. Which of the following does not belong in the role of a Scrum Master?

A. Establish priorities together with product owner for Product Backlog items

B. Preventing Senior Management from shifting team priorities

C. Empowering the team

D. Socializing scrum throughout the organization

Answer : **B**

6. What kind of information is shown in a sprint burn down chart?

A. Team Members Name

B. Number of Product Backlog Items Completed

C. Number of Tasks Remaining

D. Work Hours Remaining

Answer : **D**

7. How many hours should a member of a Scrum team work in a day?

A. A sustainable pace, usually from 7-8 hours per day.

B. An "ideal day" measuring only when he or she is productive.

C. However many hours are needed to get the work done.

D. 14 hours.

Answer : **A**

8. What is the unit of time that Scrum specifies for a team's planning of Sprint activities?

    A. Weeks

    B. Days

    C. Hours

    D. Minutes

Answer : **C**

9. As the Scrum Master, your six-person development team has finished six Sprints and has the following data:

First sprint: ten points -

Sprint 2: Eleven points -

Sprint 3: fifteen points -

Sprint 4: 14 points -

Sprint 5: 15 points -

Sprint 6: Ten pontos: There are forty-two story points left for product development. How many Sprints on average are needed to finish product development?

    A. 6

    B. 5

    C. 4

    D. 3

Answer : **B**

10. When is it appropriate to reorder the Product Backlog's priorities?

A. The Product Backlog should only be reorganized by the Scrum Master at the conclusion of each new Sprint.

B. The Product Backlog should only be reorganized by the Scrum Master at the start of each new Sprint.

C. The Product Backlog should only be reorganized by the Team at the conclusion of each new Sprint.

D. After new information is discovered, the product owner should rearrange the product backlog in order of importance.

Answer : **D**

11. How will the team and any interested parties be informed when a product backlog item is completed?

A. The member's development team should be questioned.

B. They ought to contrast what was completed with the Scrum Team's definition of done.

C. Speak with the Product Owner

D. Speak with the Manager

Answer : **B**

12. What does the daily scrum aim to achieve primarily?

A. To report progress obstacles and to share with the team what each member has finished working on throughout the Sprint.

B. To provide a status report to the Product Owner detailing each member's accomplishments during the Sprint, their upcoming tasks, and any obstacles to progress.

C. To go over work specifics with the team because everyone needs to be there for the meeting.

D. To provide a status report to the scrum master detailing each member's work performed during the sprint, what they plan to focus on going forward, and any obstacles to progress.

Answer : **A**

13. Which of the following best sums up what it means to time-box an activity?

A. A specific date must be observed for the activity to occur.

B. A specific time must be set for the activity to begin.

C. The activity has a time limit that cannot be exceeded

D. The activity has a suggested duration.

Answer : **C**

14. Which of the following best sums up the Sprint Review's main goal?

A. Presenting the Sprint work to Senior Management is the main goal of the Sprint Review.

B. Showing off the Sprint work and getting input from the Product Owner(s) on the work finished in the Sprint are the main goals of the Sprint Review.

C. The main goals of the Sprint Review are to showcase the Sprint work and get input from the Scrum Mater regarding the work that was finished in the Sprint.

D. The main goals of the Sprint Review are to present the work completed during the Sprint and offer suggestions for improving it.

Answer : **B**

15. The first sprint, of which you are the scrum master, will end in five days. In order to showcase the items finished during the sprint, you are organizing a meeting invite for the Sprint Review. Who should be invited to the Sprint Review as a mandatory attendance?

1. Owner(s) of the product

2. The Development Group

3. Users in Business

    A. 1, 2, and 3

    B. 1 and 2 only

    C. The entire company

    D. 1 only

Answer : **B**

16. The Scrum Master is you. Two days will pass until the Sprint is over. The Sprint lasts for eight hours a day. With the exception of three jobs, the team has exactly sixteen hours to finish all of the tasks. Of these three activities, one task (estimated to take two hours) is needed to complete another Product Backlog item, and two tasks (totaling six hours) are needed to complete one. What is the best way for the development team to approach the final three tasks?

A definition of "done" should be negotiated by the development team and the product owner.

B. To fulfill their obligation to the Product Owner, the development team ought to put in an additional eight hours of labor.

C. The two Product Backlog items ought to be re-added by the development team.

D. The development team ought to prioritize finishing the three items listed in the Sprint Backlog for the upcoming Sprint.

Answer : **A**

17. Which of the following best sums up the Sprint Retrospective's main goal?

A. Finding out what went wrong or prevented the sprint is the main goal of the retrospective.

B. Giving the Product Owner(s) feedback is the main goal of the Sprint Retrospective.

C. The main goal of the Sprint Retrospective is to suggest improvements for the Sprint

D. Examining the work the team performed during the sprint is the main goal of the retrospective.

Answer : **C**

18. Which of the following does a sprint burn down chart not show?

A. Total Days in Sprint

B. Number of Tasks Remaining

C. Day of Sprint

D. Work Hours Remaining

Answer : **B**

19. Which artifact contrasts planned and real progress?

    A. Work Flow

    B. Burn down Chart

    C. Task Breakdown

    D. Stakeholders

Answer : **B**

20. Which of these does not belong in the Sprint?

A. Following each Sprint, buyers can purchase the product.

B. A Sprint's main objective is to generate functionality improvements that are release-quality

C. Releases often combine the output of several Sprints

D. Occur occasionally as required by company and consumer needs

Answer : **A**

21. How much time should be spent on a sprint retrospective at most?

    A. 1 hour

    B. 1 and half hour

    C. 3 hours for a 30 day Sprint

    D. 8 hours for a 30 day Sprint

Answer : **C**

22. What occurs at the conclusion of the Sprint if all committed items (requirements) are not fulfilled?

    A. The Sprint duration is extended

    B. The tasks are determined to be unnecessary

    C. They return to the product backlog

    D. None of the above

Answer : **C**

23. The following times are the most recommended for Scrum Daily Meetings:

A. A beginning of the day

B. Immediately after lunch

C. 4:30 PM

D. 7:00 PM

Answer : **A**

24. Is Scrum Master a "management" position?

A. Yes

B. No

Answer : **A**

25. Who is on the Scrum Team?

    A. Project Manager

    B. Project Owner

    C. Product Owner

    D. Development Team

    E. Manager

    F. CEO

    G. Scrum Master

Answer : **CDG**

26. What size development team is recommended?

    A. 6, +3 or -3

    B. 9

    C. 6

    D. 7, +2 or -2

Answer : **D**

27. Who must be present at the daily scrum?

    A. Scrum Master

    B. Development Team

    C. Development Team and Product Owner

    D. Development Team and Scrum Master

Answer : **B**

28. The Development Team on a new Scrum Team informs the Scrum Master that they don't think retrospectives are necessary. Which response is accurate?

    A. Discuss with product owner

    B. Start doing retrospectives

    C. None of above

Answer : **C**

29. It is who keeps track of the Product Backlog:

   A. The Scrum Master

   B. The Development Team

   C. The Product Owner

   D. The Product Owner and Scrum Master

Answer : **C**

30. What is Scrum?

A. A framework that enables individuals to tackle intricate adaptive issues and generate highly valuable products in a creative and productive manner

B. The framework isn't agile.

C. Scrum is an all-inclusive software development process.

D. None of the preceding

Answer : **A**

31. When applying the Scrum framework, the proper order of events is as follows:

A. Sprint Review, Daily Scrum, Sprint Planning, and Sprint Retrospective

B. Sprint Review, Sprint Retrospective, Daily Scrum, Sprint Planning, and Sprint

C. Daily Scrum, Sprint Review, Sprint Planning, and Sprint Retrospective

D. Daily Scrum, Sprint, Sprint Planning, Sprint Review, and Sprint Retrospective

Answer : **B**

32. Who is able to terminate a Sprint?

A. The team members

B. The Scrum Master

C. The Product Owner

D. The Project Manager

Answer : **C**

33. The Sprint Backlog's scope is defined by who?

    A. Product Owner

    B. Development Team

    C. Scrum Master

    D. Stakeholders

Answer : **B**

34. What distinguishes the Product Backlog from the Sprint Backlog in particular?

A. The sprint backlog and the product backlog are the same.

B. The Sprint Backlog is subdivided into the Product Backlog.

C. The Product Backlog is subdivided into the Sprint Backlog.

D. The Product Owner is the owner of the Sprint Backlog.

Answer : **C**

35. The development team is no longer able to handle the increasing burden as the Sprint planning moves forward. Which course of action is best for the Team?

    A. Put in extra hours for the sprint

    B. Work with the Product Owner to remove or modify things as needed.

    C. Give up on the Sprint

    D. Lead the Sprint and assemble a larger team

Answer : **B**

36. What is included in the Sprint Backlog?

    A. User Stories, only.

    B. Use Cases

    C. Selected Backlog Items and Tasks

    D. Test cases

Answer : **C**

37. In the event that Sprint is canceled, what happens?

A. The Scrum Team instantly dissolves

B. The Product Backlog receives the entire Sprint Backlog back.

C. Items in the Sprint Backlog that are finished are assessed for release, while unfinished work is disregarded.

D. Items from the Sprint Backlog that are finished are assessed for release, and unfinished items are returned to the Product Backlog.

Answer : **D**

38. What does the burn down release mean?

A. A graph showing the tasks accomplished by the Scrum Team;

B. A measurement of the Product Backlog left over the course of a release schedule.

C. The work that the Scrum Team has finished thus far

D. The tasks that the Product Owner still has to finish

Answer : **B**

39. Who is ultimately in charge of estimating the items in the Product Backlog?

    A. The Development Team

    B. Scrum Master

    C. Stakeholders

    D. Project Owner

Answer : **D**

40. A single project or release is being worked on by multiple Scrum Teams. How should the order be for the Product Backlog?

A distinct Product Backlog is built for every Scrum Team. In an integration sprint, all of the increments are integrated at the conclusion.

B. Every Scrum Team uses the same Product Backlog and integrates their work at the end of each sprint.

C. A single Scrum Team should handle a single Scrum project.

D. Product Backlogs should be distinct for each Scrum Team.

Answer : **B**

41. Which of the following sums up what Scrum's use of the term "Sprint" means?

A sprint is a set number of days that a team uses to test and fix any problems before releasing or shipping a product.

B. A sprint is a set number of days during which a team works to complete a certain amount of work at a sustainable pace.

C. A sprint is a predetermined amount of time during which team members choose specific tasks to work on from the product backlog.

D. A sprint is a set number of days during which a team works as many hours as necessary to complete tasks that have been allocated.

Answer : **B**

42. The _____ backlog's items are subject to priority changes at any time by _____.

    A. The Team; Product

    B. The Product Owner(s); Sprint

    C. The Product Owner(s); Product

    D. The Scrum Master; Sprint

Answer : **C**

43. Which of the following doesn't belong in the Scrum cycle?

    A. Sprint retrospective

    B. Daily scrum

    C. Weekly inspection

    D. Sprint planning

Answer : **C**

44. Which of the following sums up the things in the Product Backlog the best?

> **A**. Items in the Product Backlog that are unclear or inadequately specified ought to be assigned a low priority.

> **B**. Every item in the Product Backlog is the outcome of one or more requirements, analysis, and/or design phases.

> **C**. Items in the Product Backlog that are unclear or have inadequate definitions ought to be removed until enough information is available.

> **D**. All items in the Product Backlog, regardless of priority, should have enough detail for the Team to finish working on them in a Sprint.

Answer : **C**

45. The Sprint Backlog is made up of
_____, which are frequently
approximated in hours.

    A. User Stories

    B. Use Cases

    C. Features

    D. Tasks

Answer : **D**

46. When are distinct Product Backlogs supposed to be kept up to date?

A. A single product has several Product Owners. Every Product Owner ought to possess a distinct Product Backlog.

B. Different teams are engaged on separate projects. Every distinct team and product combination ought to have its own separate Product Backlog.

C. The same team is working on several different product aspects.

D. Different teams are working on different parts of the same product. Every team ought to have its own separate Product Backlog.

Answer : **B**

47. In a sprint, who decides if the development team has been given enough work to do?

   A. The Development Team

   B. The Product Owner

   C. The Product Owner and the Scrum Master

   D. The Scrum Master

Answer : **A**

48. Which of the following is not a Product Owner responsibility?

    A. Maintaining the Product Backlog with current information

    B. Working with stakeholders to determine and detail product features

    C. Assigning tasks to team members

    D. Prioritizing the Product Backlog

Answer : **C**

49. Which of the following activities do not occur at the end of the Sprint? (Choose two)

    A. Software development

    B. Release deployment

    C. Sprint review meeting

    D. Quality assurance testing

Answer : **AD**

50. What does the Scrum Development Team strive to develop during every Sprint?

    A. A product that is ready for consumer delivery

    B. A finished Sprint Backlog

    C. A product that is ready for QA and/or QC testing

    D. A product increment that is potentially-ready for customer delivery

Answer : **D**

51. Describe the three Scrum pillars and how agility is supported by them.

_____

_____

_____

_____

_____

_____

_____

_____

_____

_____

52. Describe the Scrum Master's responsibilities within a Scrum team.

_____

_____

_____

_____

_____

_____

_____

_____

_____

_____

53. Explain the distinction between a sprint backlog and a product backlog.

_____

_____

_____

_____

_____

_____

_____

_____

_____

_____

_____

54. In what ways does Scrum encourage openness among developers?

_____

_____

_____

_____

_____

_____

_____

_____

_____

_____

_____

55. What is the Daily Scrum's objective and what kinds of questions are usually posed at this meeting?

_____

_____

_____

_____

_____

_____

_____

_____

_____

_____

56. How does the Scrum Master help the Product Owner and the development team communicate?

_____

_____

_____

_____

_____

_____

_____

_____

_____

_____

_____

57. Describe the Scrum Definition of Done and explain its significance.

_____

_____

_____

_____

_____

_____

_____

_____

_____

_____

58. Describe the idea of time-boxing in Scrum and give an illustration.

_____

_____

_____

_____

_____

_____

_____

_____

_____

_____

_____

59. How does Scrum handle requirements that change in the middle of a Sprint?

_____

_____

_____

_____

_____

_____

_____

_____

_____

_____

60. Outline the duties and role of the Product Owner within a Scrum framework.

_____

_____

_____

_____

_____

_____

_____

_____

_____

_____

_____

61. What is the purpose of a sprint review and how does it fit into the Scrum process?

_____

_____

_____

_____

_____

_____

_____

_____

_____

_____

62. How does the Scrum Master address barriers or challenges that the development team encounters?

_____

_____

_____

_____

_____

_____

_____

_____

_____

_____

_____

63. Describe the goals of the sprint retrospective and the ways in which it advances ongoing development.

_____

_____

_____

_____

_____

_____

_____

_____

_____

_____

_____

64. In Scrum, what is the purpose of a cross-functional development team?

_____

_____

_____

_____

_____

_____

_____

_____

_____

_____

65. How does Scrum manage dependencies among various projects or teams?

_____

_____

_____

_____

_____

_____

_____

_____

_____

_____

66. Explain how stakeholders fit into the Scrum framework and how their input is taken into account.

_____

_____

_____

_____

_____

_____

_____

_____

_____

_____

_____

67. How significant is the Scrum process of Product Backlog refinement?

_____

_____

_____

_____

_____

_____

_____

_____

_____

_____

_____

68. What kind of self-organization support does the Scrum Master provide to the development team?

_____

_____

_____

_____

_____

_____

_____

_____

_____

_____

69. Describe the Scrum concept of velocity and how it affects forecasting and planning.

_____

_____

_____

_____

_____

_____

_____

_____

_____

_____

_____

70. What typical anti-patterns ought a Scrum Master to recognize and deal with?

---

71. In what ways does Scrum help with risk assessment and early problem identification in a project?

_____

_____

_____

_____

_____

_____

_____

_____

_____

_____

72. Explain the Scrum Master's responsibilities during the Sprint Planning session.

_____

_____

_____

_____

_____

_____

_____

_____

_____

_____

73. How does technical debt affect Scrum, and what are some ways to manage it?

_____

_____

_____

_____

_____

_____

_____

_____

_____

_____

74. How does Scrum take emergent architecture and design into account?

_____

_____

_____

_____

_____

_____

_____

_____

_____

_____

_____

75. Describe the distinction between a project manager
and a scrum master.

_____

_____

_____

_____

_____

_____

_____

_____

_____

_____

76. How does Scrum address outside disruptions or scope modifications to the project?

_____

_____

_____

_____

_____

_____

_____

_____

_____

_____

_____

77. Explain the Development Team's involvement in Sprint Review and Sprint Planning.

_____

_____

_____

_____

_____

_____

_____

_____

_____

_____

78. In a scaled Scrum environment, what is the goal of the Scrum of Scrums meeting?

_____

_____

_____

_____

_____

_____

_____

_____

_____

_____

_____

79. What are some ways a Scrum Master can help a team foster a continuous improvement culture?

_____

_____

_____

_____

_____

_____

_____

_____

_____

_____

_____

80. Describe the function of Scrum's Definition of Ready and how it affects Sprint Planning.

_____

_____

_____

_____

_____

_____

_____

_____

_____

81. How do product roadmaps and long-term planning fit into Scrum?

_____

_____

_____

_____

_____

_____

_____

_____

_____

_____

_____

82. Explain how a Scrum Master helps to settle disputes within the team.

_____

_____

_____

_____

_____

_____

_____

_____

_____

_____

_____

83. What does it mean at the conclusion of each Sprint to have a "potentially shippable product increment"?

_____

_____

_____

_____

_____

_____

_____

_____

_____

_____

_____

84. How does Scrum handle the requirement for documentation in projects involving software development?

_____

_____

_____

_____

_____

_____

_____

_____

_____

_____

_____

85. Describe servant leadership and how it relates to the Scrum Master position.

---

86. Explain how Scrum differs from other Agile frameworks (like Kanban).

_____

_____

_____

_____

_____

_____

_____

_____

_____

_____

87. What are some ways a Scrum Master can encourage cooperation between stakeholders and team members?

_____

_____

_____

_____

_____

_____

_____

_____

_____

_____

88. How does a Scrum Master ensure that the team follows the Scrum framework?

_____

_____

_____

_____

_____

_____

_____

_____

_____

_____

89. How does Scrum manage team composition changes that occur during a project?

---

90. Describe "Inspect and Adapt" in the framework of Scrum.

_____

_____

_____

_____

_____

_____

_____

_____

_____

_____

_____

91. How does a Scrum team's performance depend on its technical prowess?

_____

_____

_____

_____

_____

_____

_____

_____

_____

_____

92. How can a Scrum Master assist a team in handling deadline pressure and outside influences?

_____

_____

_____

_____

_____

_____

_____

_____

_____

_____

93. Explain how the Scrum Master promotes a positive team culture and manages team dynamics.

_____

_____

_____

_____

_____

_____

_____

_____

_____

_____

94. How does Scrum deal with the difficulty of planning and estimating for complicated tasks?

_____

_____

_____

_____

_____

_____

_____

_____

_____

_____

95. What are the main Agile Manifesto tenets, and how do they relate to Scrum values?

---

96. How can a Scrum Master help a remote or distributed team communicate more effectively?

_____

_____

_____

_____

_____

_____

_____

_____

_____

_____

_____

97. Explain how a scrum master helps a project maintain a balance between predictability and flexibility.

_____

_____

_____

_____

_____

_____

_____

_____

_____

_____

98. In what ways does Scrum facilitate the ideas of continuous integration and continuous delivery?

_____

_____

_____

_____

_____

_____

_____

_____

_____

_____

99. How is the Sprint Burndown chart used in Scrum, and what is its significance?

_____

_____

_____

_____

_____

_____

_____

_____

_____

_____

_____

100. How can a Scrum Master help a team switch from using the traditional project management methodology to using the Scrum framework?

_____

_____

_____

_____

_____

_____

_____

_____

_____

_____

Made in United States
Orlando, FL
18 October 2024

52825778R00065